Table of Contents

This Book

This book was written to explain how to plan an online presence. Visit http://www.DivStart.com for more information and resources.

Copyright

Trademarks

Disclaimer

Introduction

Thank you for purchasing this book. The goal of this book is to help you take your ideas for websites, software, social networking applications, and/or iPhone applications, and to help you refine your ideas and document these ideas so that you have descriptions and drawings you can refer to when you develop them. This book does not explain how to program to develop these websites, social networking applications, and/or iPhone applications.

This book could have discussed how to plan a particular type of website, social networking application, and/or iPhone application. However, I do not want to pin this book or these steps down to developing a particular type of application because with the growth of the web and the development of an ever increasing number of new technologies, it is important to consider launching your application or parts of your application on different platforms and through different distribution channels.

This book starts off with a list of seven steps to plan an online business. Each step is explained in order throughout this book. Worksheets are provided for each step so you can document your ideas. I suggest you either photocopy these worksheets, write your answers to the questions on the worksheets in this book (if you are only going to use these worksheets once), write your answers to these questions on your own paper, or write your answers to these questions in a text document on your computer. It is important to document your ideas.

Best of Luck Planning An Online Business!

– John Cook

Start Planning Online Businesses
In 7 Steps

The 7 Steps

1	Assess Your Situation
2	Brainstorm Niches
3	Generate Ideas
4	Research Ideas
5	Determine Feasibility
6	Document for Development
7	Obtain Domain Name and Website Hosting

1. Assess Your Situation

Start with your situation. What do you have?

- Do you already have an offline business?
- Are you working with a charity or other nonprofit organization?
- Are you a real estate agent, insurance salesperson, or are you in a similar occupation?
- Are you trying to get elected?
- Are you trying to create a website to showcase your skills to try to get a job?
- Would an online presence help a project you are working on?
- Do you already have an online presence that you want to change or improve?
- Can your hobby be turned into a business?
- Do you have an idea for a business?

Now, brainstorm goals that you want to achieve.

General Goals

Example goals include:

- Making money
- Getting online orders through a web-based e-commerce solution
- Providing information to website visitors
- Getting phone calls
- Acquiring sales leads
- Receiving emails
- Acquiring newsletter subscribers
- Obtaining referrals

Situation Specific Goals

There are also situation specific goals. Example goals include:

Goals for people with offline businesses:

- To get people to visit your store
- To advertise/brand your company

Goals for real estate professionals:

- To display clients' homes

- To provide real estate information

- To provide a service for your hometown

Goals for non-profit organizations:

- To generate awareness

- To get volunteers

- To get donations

Goals for politicians:

- To get donations

- To get elected

- To get volunteers

Goals for portfolio websites:

- To advertise/brand yourself

- To get a job

Goals for hobby websites:

- To provide a discussion board

- To provide hobby related information

- To host images/video/etc... about your hobby/club

See if any of these goals apply to you and try to think of your own goals. At this point it is not necessary to get extremely specific. For example, you do not have to specify a dollar amount that you want to earn in a specific time frame doing specific activities. The purpose of step one is for you to get a general idea of the goal or goals of your online presence. Add to your goal or goals as you continue through this book. You can get more specific in later steps.

Assess Your Situation Example

What is your situation? What do you have?

Possible answers to this question could include, among other things, already owning a business or that you have an interest in starting a business.

What general goals do you have?

Possible answers to this question could include, among other things, making money, getting newsletter subscribers, or providing information to website visitors.

What goals do you have that are specific to your situation?

A possible answer to this question could be getting people to visit your offline store.

Assess Your Situation Worksheet

What is your situation? What do you have? (Circle One)

- Already have an offline business

- Working with a charity or non-profit organization

- In a sales occupation

- Want to turn a hobby into a business

- Want to create an online portfolio

- Want to improve your existing online presence

- Other (Describe Below)

_____

What general goals do you have?

_____

_____

_____

What goals do you have that are specific to your situation?

_____

_____

_____

_____

2. Brainstorm Niches

The goal of this part is to generate a list of possible niches.

If you want to start an online business but do not have any idea what your niche could be try to identify:

- Your hobbies, skills and/or talents
- Your professional experience
- Industries/markets that interest you
- Information you learned in school/college
- What you know how to manufacture or make
- Things you can buy cheap and sell for more money
- Other information that you know

You can also try to find a random niche by:

- Looking for popular trends online and finding related niches. To do this you could use:

- Google Insights (http://www.google.com/insights/search/)

- Yahoo Buzz Index (http://buzzlog.buzz.yahoo.com/overall/)

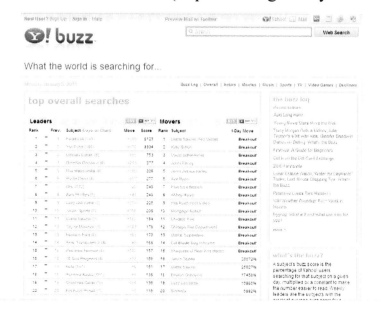

- Walking through various larger department stores, home improvement stores, book stores, or other stores and looking at the products on the shelves and trying to identify these products' niches. You could ask store managers or store salespeople which products are popular.

- Asking friends, family members, or anyone else you know what they are interested in and what they buy.

Write down as many ideas as you can. You can use your answers to these questions to help you find a niche.

Niches can be general or specific.

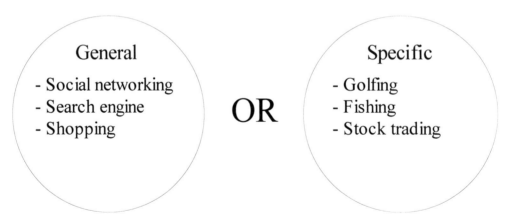

General
- Social networking
- Search engine
- Shopping

OR

Specific
- Golfing
- Fishing
- Stock trading

Websites like search engines or social networks can be considered general niches because it is difficult to identify a specific situation, profession, activity, interest, hobby or other unifying thing to group most individuals in this general niche together. For example, you can not assume that a large majority of people who use a search engine like to play table tennis. General niches have advantages and disadvantages.

The advantages of a general niche may include:
- A large audience/market
- Potential to become large

The disadvantages of a general niche may include:
- Higher start up costs
- Harder to advertise/market
- Harder to manage growth

When thinking of specific niches, realize that there are different divisions of specific niches ranging from most general to most specific. A specific niche might both be a part of another larger specific niche and contain smaller more specific niches. For example, while you might consider stock trading to be a specific niche, realize that stock trading is a part of the larger niche of investing and that stock trading could be broken down into smaller niches depending on:
- The size of the companies
    - Penny stocks

- Small caps
- Mid caps
- Large caps
- The level of risk
  - High risk
  - Moderate risk
  - Low risk
- The type of stock trader
  - Retired and managing own portfolio
  - Professional stock trader
  - Casual stock trader
- Amount of money invested
  - $50,000,000+
  - $1,000,000 - $49,999,999
  - $250,000 - $999,999
  - $100,000 - $249,999
  - Under $100,000
- Other things

When thinking about your niche, consider both the larger niche or niches that your niche could be a component of and the smaller niches that are within your niche. Depending on how many people you can advertise to or market to in your niche and how competitive your niche is, you might want to either expand to focus on the larger niche or you might want to narrow your focus to a smaller niche. One way to get ideas for smaller niches is to visit internet discussion boards or forums centered around your larger niche idea. On these forums people will be discussing more specific topics, which may be potential niches. To find these forums, you could search the internet for the name of your niche followed by the word forum or the word vBulletin.

When compared to general niches, specific niches have advantages and disadvantages.

The advantages of a specific niche may include:
- Easier to start
- Easier to manage

The disadvantages of a specific niche may include:
- Limited income potential
  (However you could overcome this by focusing on broader specific niches or with multiple online presences in multiple niches.)

To find a random niche, you could walk through various larger department stores, home improvement stores, or other stores and look at the products on the shelves. As you look at a specific product or a specific category of products, think about the problems that people might be having that would cause them to buy that product or those products. You could also think about the type of person who would be buying those products and think of what other problems they might be facing.

Fill out the worksheet at the end of this step multiple times, once for each niche idea. If there are niches that you know you will not do anything with no matter what, then you can eliminate them.

Brainstorm Niches Example

Choose A Niche: Tennis   **This Niche is:** Specific

How is this niche applicable to you? A typical answer to this question could be that you own a business in this niche, or that you have an interest in this niche.

Do you currently sell any products or services in this niche? No

Why do you want an online presence in this niche? A typical answer to this question could include that the niche is profitable, you can think of a unique way of connecting users within the niche, or a similar reason.

Brainstorm Niches Worksheet

Niche Name:

_____

This Niche is: General / Specific   (Circle One)

How is this niche applicable to you?

_____

_____

_____

_____

_____

Do you currently sell any products or services in this niche?

Yes / No
(Circle One)

Why do you want an online presence in this niche?

_____

_____

_____

_____

_____

3. Generate Ideas

The goal of this step is to take your niches and generate ideas. This step starts by mentioning various monetization strategies and distribution channels. You should then create a spreadsheet where you can input the ideas you develop in this step.

Monetization Strategies

Monetization strategies are described over the next few pages.

Monetization strategy resources such as links to companies that can provide you with advertisements to put on your website, are available at http://www.divstart.com/resources/monetization

Products

There are physical and digital products.

Physical products include:

- products that you make
- products that your business already sells
- reselling imported products

Digital products include:

- Information products such as:
  - eBooks
  - Video tutorials
  - Audio books/tutorials
  - Interactive tutorials/ instructional software
- Downloadable music (mp3s)
- Virtual goods such as:
  - Currency within a game
  - Website credits
  - Businesses within second life

Services

Services include:

- Services provided by you or your company such as:

  - Consulting

  - Software development

- Services provided through a website that involves payment in exchange for completing one automated task like taking a video file and converting it to different formats or something similar. However, if it involves payment for access to the website for a certain period of time, then it is a subscription.

Subscriptions

Subscriptions are recurring payments by website users in exchange for things like:

- Information products delivered on a regular basis
- Physical products mailed on a regular basis (ex: monthly)
- Services provided by you or your company on a regular basis
- Access to services provided by a website for a set amount of time

Affiliate Marketing

Affiliate marketing is the promotion of other companies products, services, and subscriptions in exchange for compensation if anyone that you referred to that company buys something.

If you are interested in affiliate marketing, you should search for affiliate programs in your niche. Try to find companies who have affiliate programs and are either in your niche or are targeting a similar demographic to your niche's demographic by searching the internet for the name of your niche followed by either "affiliate programs" or "associate programs".

Advertising

You could sell ads. You have the option of managing the sales of these ads or getting your ads from another company who finds the advertisers, gives you code to put on your web pages, and possibly pays you after these ads are either displayed and/or clicked on.

Donations

If you are a non-profit organization, you could accept donations through your website.

You could also possibly use a website like http://www.kickstarter.com to use donations to raise money for a project.

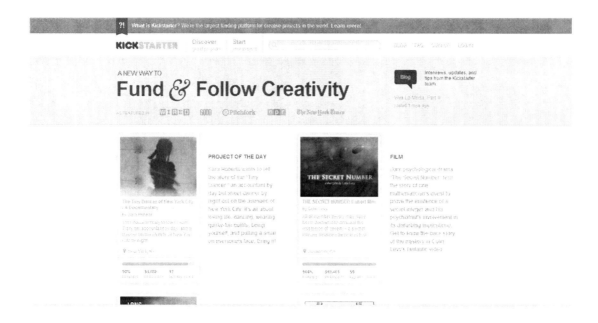

Distribution Channels

There are several different distribution channels, which will be described in the next few pages. It is important to keep in mind that you can choose more than one distribution channel and that some distribution channels are better suited than others to various monetization strategies.

Distribution channel resources such as names of certain types of web applications and links to their websites are available at http://www.divstart.com/resources/distribution

A Static Website

A static website is a website consisting of basic web pages. Static websites do not use databases to store information such as user login information, user profile information, or website content.

The main disadvantage of a static website is that there is not a database behind the website to enable more powerful features such as searching the website's content or easily displaying hundreds or thousands of products.

More Suited To:
- Listing maybe 1 to 20 physical products
- Listing maybe 1 to 20 affiliate products
- Listing maybe 1 to 20 services offered offline
- Displaying ads where another company manages finding the advertisers and provides you with code to put on your website
- Receiving donations where a donate button is placed on your website, but another company processes payments

An advantage of a static website is that it will probably cost the least to develop.

Web Applications

A web application is a dynamic website that usually has more features than a static website.

Examples of web applications include:

- Search engines
- Social networking websites
- E-commerce websites

There are existing web applications available online that you can customize and use or you can develop your own.

With custom developed web applications, you can use just about any monetization strategy, and combine monetization strategies in ways that you see fit.

A WordPress website, a blog, and a forum/discussion board are all examples of web applications.

A WordPress Website

WordPress is a web application that is flexible, enabling you to have both blog posts and regular web pages on your site. Additionally, it allows you to edit the website's posts, pages, design, title and other settings from web-based pages accessible to logged in website administrators. WordPress is open source software that is available from www.wordpress.org for free.

More Suited To:

- Displaying affiliate products
- Displaying ads where another company manages finding the advertisers and provides you with code to put on your website
- Receiving donations where a donate button is placed on the website, but another company processes payments

With Plugins:

- Displaying products
- Displaying services
- Offering subscriptions

A Blog

If you want to provide advice, reviews, and other relevant information, adding a blog may help bring visitors to your website. If you update the blog fairly frequently (daily or at least once every couple days), a blog may provide reasons for visitors to come to your website and keep visiting your website.

More suited to:
- Displaying affiliate products
- Displaying ads where another company manages finding the advertisers and provides you with code to put on your website
- Receiving donations where a donate button is placed on the website, but another company processes payments

With Plugins/Modifications:
- Displaying products
- Displaying services
- Offering subscriptions

A Forum/Discussion Board

A forum/discussion board allows users to communicate with one another. It can be used to attract visitors and keep them coming back to post and read other people's responses to their posts.

You can:

- Sell subscriptions
- Sell information products
- Display affiliate products
- Display ads where another company manages finding the advertisers and provides you with code to put on your website
- Receive donations where a donate button is placed on the website, but another company processes payments

With modifications you might be able to:

- List products/services for sale

Keep in mind that a forum is a live community. Your forum members may feel like they have a stake in your forum. You may experience backlash if you delete too many negative comments about your company, or do other forms of censoring. You need to state the rules and reach a balance with forum members as to what will be censored.

Hosted Shopping Applications

There are services that make it easier for you to sell products online. These services are mostly focused around selling physical products online, and usually enable you to log in, modify settings, add product information, and sell products.

Social Networking Applications

Social Networking applications like FaceBook applications help users connect with their friends on FaceBook. By developing FaceBook applications, you can possibly get in front of an audience and get FaceBook users to virally promote your message to their friends.

For example, if you can embed your message into a game that FaceBook users want to play with their friends, or do something else innovative and your app takes off, it can be very beneficial to you.

Just like custom developed web applications, social networking applications can use just about any monetization strategy, and monetization strategies can be combined in ways that you see fit.

Phone Applications

Phone applications such as iPhone applications are installed to users' iPhones and they enable users to do more with their iPhones. iPhone applications can be sold or available for free through the App store. You can also embed ads into your apps.

Phone applications can use just about any monetization strategy. However, you can not currently accept donations through iPhone applications or use the money generated from the sale of iPhone applications as donations.

Consider that several successful websites have elements that make it easier for these websites to become a part of someone's life. What does this mean? People keep visiting the website, reading its content, buying products from it, and interacting with it because of the way it is designed.

Existing websites try to do this by:
- being interactive and enabling people to communicate with others in a forum
- providing a service that people want to use on a daily basis
- offering a monthly subscription to a members area that's updated with new content fairly often

Some distribution channels are better suited to these kinds of elements than other distribution channels.

I suggest you now create a spreadsheet for each of your niche ideas. In this spreadsheet, rows are distribution channels and columns are monetization strategies.

You can create this spreadsheet in Microsoft Excel or another software program. If you do not have Microsoft Excel, you could use OpenOffice.org Calc, an open source alternative to Microsoft Excel. For more information about OpenOffice.org Calc, visit http://www.openoffice.org

To organize your spreadsheets (one for each niche), you can either keep multiple spreadsheets in one file or you can store all of your spreadsheets as separate files in one folder on your computer.

Not every distribution channel or monetization strategy will probably apply to you. For example, the donations monetization strategy might not be applicable to a for profit business. Fill in the cells that apply to you with information about how you would use that channel and that monetization strategy together. For example, what products would you sell on a static website? Are there any affiliate programs you could promote through a web application? Leave the cells that do not apply to you blank.

Generate Ideas Example

While you can put your ideas into the spreadsheet itself, because of limited space for this example, I am going to put letters in the spreadsheet and then explain these letters below the spreadsheet.

Tennis Niche	Products	Services	Subscriptions	Affiliate	Advertising	Donations
Web						
Website		J				
Web Application	B		S			
WordPress				AB		
FaceBook App						
A Blog					AL	
A Forum						
Hosted Shop	G					
Software						
Desktop						
Phone						
iPhone App						

B. Tennis Information Products

eBooks about tennis, tennis books, tennis audio products, tennis training software, and/or tennis videos are all possibilities.

G. Physical Tennis Products

Physical tennis products like tennis racquets, tennis balls, ball hoppers, and tennis shoes could be sold. In your case, if you had a product catalog, you could mention it here.

J. Offline Tennis Services

Offline tennis services could include access to a tennis facility for a certain period time and/or tennis lessons.

S. Tennis Members Area

An online members area could be set up to provide information, videos, a members only discussion area, audio information, access to eBooks, and/or other things.

AB. Affiliate Products

Affiliate products in the tennis niche could be mentioned and linked to.

AL. Ads

Ads could be displayed.

Generate Ideas Example

Documenting Each Idea

Niche Name	Letter	Channel Name	Monetization Strategy
Tennis	G	Hosted Shop	Products

Describe Your Idea

You could mention how you plan on using a hosted shop to sell physical tennis products.

Potential External Services   (Ex: Ad networks, Affiliate programs)

You can probably leave this section blank for this channel and monetization strategy.

Products/Info Products/Services/Subscriptions

Name	Tennis Racquet	Tennis Shoes
Description	A part number could be listed here.	A part number could be listed here.
Price	$ Price	$ Price

Generate Ideas Worksheet

Start with a spreadsheet like the one below. Add your ideas to each cell of the spreadsheet that is applicable to you.

Niche Name	Products	Services	Subscriptions	Affiliate	Advertising	Donations
Web						
Website	A	J		Z	AH	AQ
Web Application	B	K	S	AA	AI	AR
WordPress	C	L	T	AB	AJ	AS
FaceBook App	D	M	U	AC	AK	AT
A Blog	E	N	V	AD	AL	AU
A Forum	F	O	W	AE	AM	AV
Hosted Shop	G	P			AN	
Software						
Desktop	H	Q	X	AF	AO	AW
Phone						
iPhone App	I	R	Y	AG	AP	

Generate Ideas Worksheet

Documenting Each Idea

Niche Name   Letter   Channel Name   Monetization Strategy

_____   _____   _____   _____

Describe Your Idea

_____

_____

Potential External Services   **(Ex: Ad networks, Affiliate programs)**

_____

_____

Products/Info Products/Services/Subscriptions

<u>Name</u>   _____   _____

<u>Description</u>   _____   _____

              _____   _____

<u>Price</u>   _____   _____

4. Research Ideas

Now that you have niche ideas, you can do market research to determine if a market exists for your ideas.

Before starting, think about what makes a niche a good niche. This goes back to your goals. If your goal is to make money, then a good niche would have lots of customers and few small competitors. Also consider that even if your niche has lots of competitors, if you know of a way to get customers that the competitors are not using, then you have a chance as long as your competitors do not dilute the effectiveness of your method of getting customers and as long as your method of getting customers is legal and ethical.

To see if a niche meets these conditions, we will first do competition research to see what is out there. Then we will do market research to see how large these competitors are, who the target customer is, the competitiveness of the niche, and the size of the niche.

Competition Research

Add information about competitors below your niche ideas in the spreadsheet you created in the last step. Try to find a few competitors for each distribution channel and monetization strategy. You can visit http://www.xmarks.com and type in the URL of a competitor's website to find other competitors that are similar to that competitor.

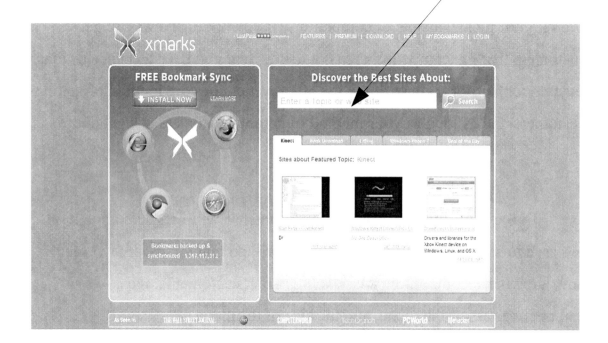

Competitor websites are listed under the section titled Similar Sites.

In each cell in the spreadsheet, write the following information for each company you find:

- The name of the company

- The company's website URL

- The name of the specific project/website that uses that distribution channel and that monetization strategy

- What you like about it

- What you dislike about it

You should be able to find this information through general internet searches. If one company belongs in more than one cell, then you can write the name of the company and the name of the specific project/website that uses that distribution channel and that monetization strategy in all of the cells that the company could fit into. Then randomly choose one of these cells that it could fit into to put more details about the company.

Market Research

Now that you have a general idea of the competition for each niche, you can get more specific and look at:

- Size of competitors
- The target customer
- Search competition
- Niche size

Size of Competitors

Visit http://www.compete.com and enter the website URL of each competitor you found in the last step.

For each competitor in each niche add the following below the other information for that competitor in the appropriate cell in the spreadsheet:

- The Current Monthly Unique Visitors
- The Highest Monthly Unique Visitors (Past 12 Months)
- The Lowest Monthly Unique Visitors (Past 12 Months)

If the number is not displayed on the screen, hover your mouse over the dots on the chart.

Visit http://www.jigsaw.com and enter the webiste URL of each competitor.

For each competitor in each niche add the number of employees and the revenue estimate underneath the other information for that competitor in the appropriate cell in the spreadsheet.

The Target Customer

Visit http://www.alexa.com and enter the website URL of each competitor.

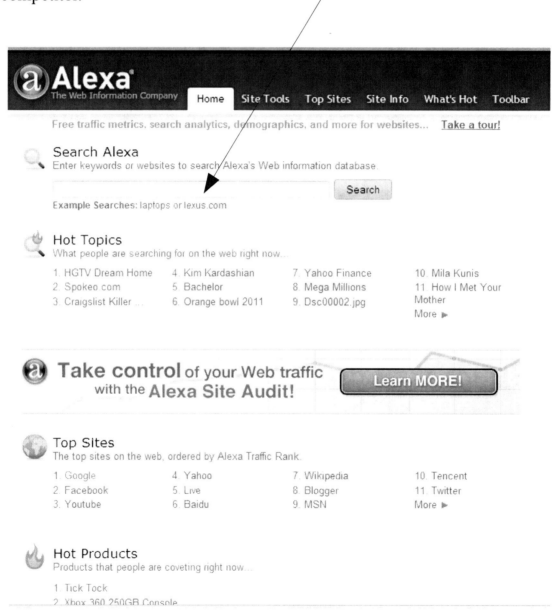

You will then see the search results page. Site information is shown at the top of the search results. Click on get details.

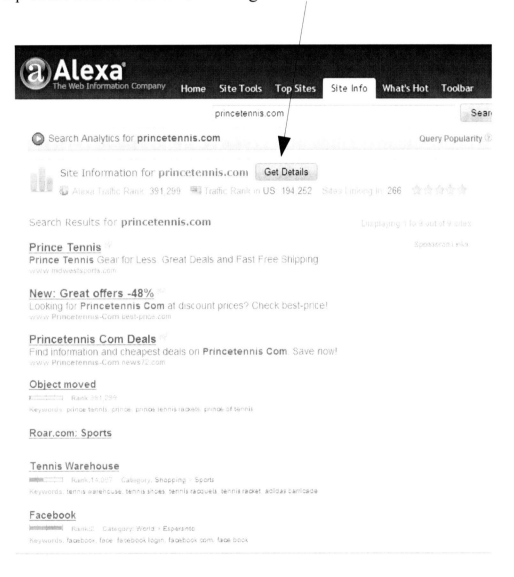

The details for that website appear. The Alexa Traffic Rank is a popularity ranking, where the websites on the internet are compared and ranked based on the number of visitors each website receives. The website with the most visitors has an Alexa Traffic Rank of 1 and lower numbered rankings are better.

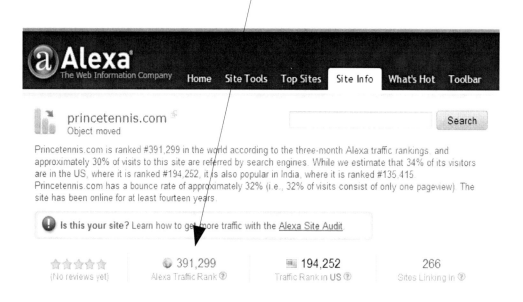

For each competitor in each niche add the following underneath the other information for that competitor in the appropriate cell in the spreadsheet.

- The countries listed under the section for that website's worldwide traffic rank

Click on the audience tab.

- Type over-represented and list the over-represented:
  - Gender
  - Age ranges
  - Education demographics
  - Child status
  - Browsing locations
- Type under-represented and list the under-represented:
  - Gender
  - Age ranges
  - Education demographics
  - Child status
  - Browsing locations

Search Competition

While you are still on http://www.alexa.com and still looking at information about each competitor, click on the search analytics tab.

Scroll down to the high impact search queries section. For each competitor in each niche add the word keywords followed by a list of keywords that have a high query popularity and a low QCI underneath the other information for that competitor in the appropriate cell in the spreadsheet. Beside each keyword put the numbers provided for that keyword's query popularity and that keyword's QCI.

Niche Size

For each of the competitors, look at the queries that have the highest query popularity regardless of the QCI. Visit https://adwords.google.com/select/KeywordToolExternal and enter these keywords to get estimates for the global monthly searches.

For each competitor in each niche add the phrase popular keywords followed by a list of keywords that have a high query popularity underneath the other information for that competitor in the appropriate cell in the spreadsheet. Beside these keywords, make note of the number of global monthly searches.

Additionally, try to think of other popular keywords for the niche and enter those into the keyword tool and the niche spreadsheets. If you need help coming up with synonyms you can visit http://www.visuwords.com

Enter words into the box.

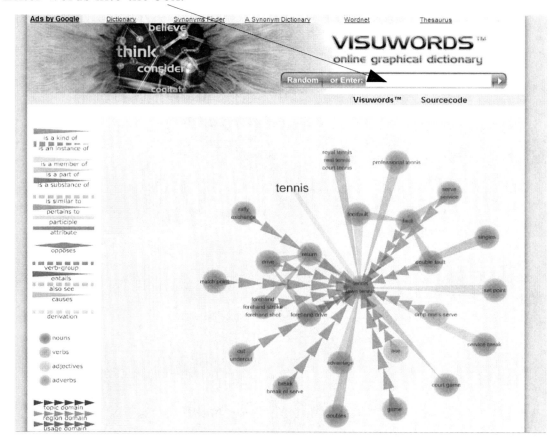

For all of these keywords, see if there is an article for each of them on http://www.wikipedia.org and if there is check the traffic to that specific Wikipedia page by visiting http://stats.grok.se/ Make note of a common daily traffic number to that page in your spreadsheets. For example if most of the traffic numbers to a page range from 40,000 visitors a day to 60,000 visitors a day, 50,000 visitors a day is an estimate.

After entering the name of a wikipedia article title, the results are displayed.

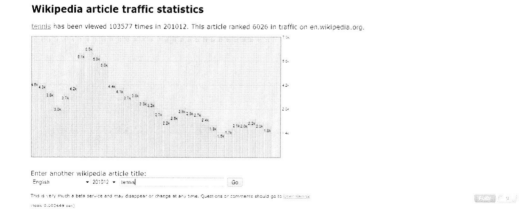

Also, for all of these keywords, see if there is a group or a page about it on Facebook. http://www.facebook.com If there is, make note of the number of group members or page likes in your spreadsheets.

Research Ideas Example

This example builds on the example and worksheet from the previous step. You should already have a spreadsheet that looks similar to the one below.

Niche Name	Products	Services	Subscriptions	Affiliate	Advertising	Donations
Web						
Website	A	J		Z	AH	AQ
Web Application	B	K	S	AA	AI	AR
WordPress	C	L	T	AB	AJ	AS
FaceBook App	D	M	U	AC	AK	AT
A Blog	E	N	V	AD	AL	AU
A Forum	F	O	W	AE	AM	AV
Hosted Shop	G	P			AN	
Software						
Desktop	H	Q	X	AF	AO	AW
Phone						
iPhone App	I	R	Y	AG	AP	

Now, add to the documentation for each idea in each cell of this spreadsheet.

Research Ideas Example

Researching Each Competitor for Each Idea

Niche Name	Letter	Channel Name	Monetization Strategy
<u>Tennis</u>	<u>B</u>	<u>Web App</u>	<u>Products</u>

Competitor: **Number: <u>1</u>**   **(For This Channel & Monetization)**

<u>Prince Sports Inc.</u>

<u>http://www.princetennis.com/</u>

<u>Prince Tennis Website</u>

Likes:

- Navigation menu
- Racquet selector

Dislikes:

- Website is coded in Adobe Flash
  - Flash websites can not be viewed on the iPhone.
  - Search engines may have problems understanding the content on Flash websites.

Size of Competitors:

According to compete.com statistics from January 1st, 2011:

Current Monthly Unique Visitors: 6,335

Highest Monthly Unique Visitors: 15,246

Lowest Monthly Unique Visitors: 2,858

According to jigsaw.com statistics from January 1st, 2011:

For Prince Sports, Inc. ← Prince Tennis is a part of this.

Number of employees: 250 – 1,000

Revenue: $50 – 100 Million

The Target Customer:

Top Countries:

<u>India, United States</u>

Over-represented:

Gender:	Male
Age Ranges:	35 - 44
Education Demographics:	College, Graduate School
Child Status:	Yes
Browsing Locations:	Work

Under-represented:

Gender:	Female
Age Ranges:	18 – 24, 25 – 34, 45 – 54
Education Demographics:	No college, Some college
Child Status:	No
Browsing Locations:	Home

Search Competition:

Information obtained from Alexa, Google's external keyword tool, http://stats.grok.se and Facebook on January 1st, 2011.

keyword (Query Popularity, QCI)	Searches	PageViews	Likes
prince (55, 17)	16,600,000		25,849
tennis (54, 40)	16,600,000	4,000	2,358,062

Niche Size:

tennis shoes (34, 57)	246,000	28	824
tennis rackets (32, 61)	246,000	< 1	55

Research Ideas Worksheet

Niche Name   Letter   Channel Name   Monetization Strategy

_____   _____   _____   _____

Competitor: **Number: _____**   **(For This Channel & Monetization)**

Company Name: _____

Company URL: _____

Project Name: _____

Likes:

_____

_____

Dislikes:

_____

_____

Size of Competitors:

Current Monthly Unique Visitors: _____

Highest Monthly Unique Visitors: _____

Lowest Monthly Unique Visitors: _____

Number of employees: _____

Revenue: _____

Comments/Opinion on Competition Size:

_____

_____

_____

_____

The Target Customer:

Top Countries:

_____

_____

Over-represented (Circle Applicable)

Gender: Male   Female

Age Ranges: 18 – 24   25 – 34   35 – 44   45 – 54

Education Demographics:

     No college   Some College   College   Graduate School

Child Status: Yes   No

Browsing Locations: Home   Work

Under-represented (Circle Applicable)

Gender: Male   Female

Age Ranges: 18 – 24   25 – 34   35 – 44   45 – 54

Education Demographics:

     No college   Some College   College   Graduate School

Child Status: Yes   No

Browsing Locations: Home   Work

Search Competition:

Keyword (Query Popularity, QCI) Searches   PageViews   Likes

_____

_____

_____

_____

_____

Niche Size:

_____

_____

_____

_____

5. Determine Feasibility

While this step will try to provide you with suggestions on how you could possibly determine feasibility, you have to make the final decision. There is no magic formula; you have to make a decision based on the information you have. Also keep in mind that you can have multiple websites in multiple niches, but I suggest you start with one niche and develop it first before moving on.

To Determine Feasibility:

- Look for opportunities
- Determine which opportunities you can pursue
- Determine whether they are worth your time
- Choose one

Look for opportunities

Analyze the spreadsheet for each niche and try to determine if there are any gaps in what the market is asking for and what is currently being offered by competitors.

These spreadsheets should now contain information about:
- Your ideas for the niche
- Competition within the niche
- The size of the niche

If opportunities are not obvious, I would look through each cell within a niche spreadsheet to see how the competition is aligned to the size of the niche. Is there a channel and a monetization strategy that is not being used by most of the competition but has a large market?

Also remember that niches can be broken down into divisions ranging from most general to most specific. You could try to find opportunities within more general or more specific niches.

Determine which opportunities you can pursue

Now, on to feasibility. There is more to feasibility than whether or not there is a market for your ideas within a niche. You also need to consider whether or not you can develop and promote your ideas. Additionally you need to consider whether or not you can justify spending the resources you need to spend to develop and promote your ideas.

However, before discussing how to determine which opportunities you can pursue, it is important to first understand how websites work.

To have a website online, you need:
- A domain name
- Website hosting
- The website's files

If your website is a web application, you might also need access to a database through your website hosting.

While domain names and website hosting are covered in step 7, I will briefly describe them here.

The domain name is the URL (Uniform Resource Locator). Domain names consist of the name and the extension which is usually .com .org or something similar.

Website hosting is used to host your website's files. There are different types of website hosting depending on what type of website you want to host, the type of content on your website (text, audio, video, etc...) and how many people visit your website every month. To determine what type of website hosting you need for your projects visit http://www.divstart.com/resources/hosting

Your website's files are uploaded to your website hosting, web applications are setup/installed and your website is online.

Free Information

Some website owners post information to various distribution channels and to various websites across the internet with a link back to their website and enable people to view this information for free. Why do they do this?

They do this because they think it might help them build trust with their niche market. Ideally, people read their information, find it valuable, start to trust the website owner, and possibly buy something from them.

The Email Newsletter

You have probably visited websites that ask you to subscribe to an email newsletter. In exchange for subscribing, you may have been offered a free report, a coupon for a discount off the price of a product on the website, access to a members area on the website, and/or something else. Think about it. Why would a website owner offer you something in exchange for subscribing to his or her newsletter?

Consider that usually most visitors to a website leave that website, do not buy anything, and never come back. This is one reason why website owners try to get website visitors to at least subscribe to a newsletter to show their possible interest. If a website owner has a website visitor's email address and permission to email that website visitor, that website owner can follow up and try to get a sale later.

Squeeze Pages

Some website owners like to use squeeze pages to present information and ask the website visitor to subscribe to an email newsletter to receive more information for free. These squeeze pages are usually very uncluttered, including maybe a video, a link to a PDF, or text information and a box to subscribe to an email newsletter. At the bottom of the page, there are also links to legal documents such as terms of service. A website visitor can quickly look at this page and figure out what the website is about.

Keep the previously mentioned information in mind when determining feasibility, because, for example, if you are interested in using squeeze pages, you might need an autoresponder email service. More information about autoresponders can be found at http://www.divstart.com/resources/email

It will take time and money to develop your projects. In order to determine whether a project is feasible, you need to come up with an estimate of the time and money required. Thus, an overview of the steps required to develop a project within each distribution channel follows to give you a better idea of what might be required. You may want to outsource some of the steps required. More information about outsourcing can be found at http://www.divstart.com/resources/outsourcing and don't forget about http://www.divstart.com/resources/distribution for information specific to each distribution channel.

A Static Website

A static website is a website consisting of basic web pages. Static websites do not use databases to store information such as user login information, user profile information, or website content.

To develop a static website, you can:
- Start from scratch
- Start with a website template

If you are starting from scratch, you need to:
- Create the HTML files for the content of the website
- Possibly create CSS files for the design of the website
- Obtain images for the website

If you are starting with a website template, you need to:
- Modify the HTML/CSS files and images that came with the website template

To see website templates available for sale, visit http://www.divstart.com/resources/templates

For the website images, you can:

- Use a digital camera and/or graphics software to create these images yourself
- Find images on stock photography websites that you can use on your website
- Modify or use the images included with a website template
- Hire someone else to use a digital camera and/or graphics software to create these images

For more information about stock photography websites, visit http://www.divstart.com/resources/images

You also need to know how to upload your HTML, CSS, and image files to your website hosting.

You can do these things yourself, or you can outsource them.

Web Applications

A web application is a dynamic website that usually has more features than a static website.

Examples of web applications include:
- Search engines
- Social networking websites
- E-commerce websites

To develop a web application, you can:
- Modify an existing web application
- Write your own web application from scratch

To modify a web application you need to:
- Find an existing web application
- Find out what programming language it is coded in:
  - PHP
  - Ruby on Rails
  - ASP
  - Other languages

- Download the web application's files
- Modify the web application's files:
  - You can modify these files yourself if you are familiar with the programming language that was used to code it.
  - You can outsource the modification of these files.
- Determine whether you need to modify the structure of the web application's database and if necessary, modify it or outsource its modification.

To write your own web application you need to:
- Decide on a programming language
  - PHP (I usually go with PHP.)
  - Ruby on Rails
  - ASP
  - Other languages
- Start with your documentation plan and start coding. You can:
  - Program your web application yourself if you are familiar with the programming language that you decided to use to code it.
  - Outsource the programming of the web application.
- You might also need to create images. You can:

82

- Use a digital camera and/or graphics software to create these images yourself
- Find images on stock photography websites that you can use on your website
- Modify or use the images included with a website template
- Hire someone else to use a digital camera and/or graphics software to create these images

Whether you modify an existing web application or you develop your own, you also need to know how to:

- Upload your web application's files
- Install/setup your web application

A WordPress Website

WordPress is a web application that is flexible, enabling you to have both blog posts and regular web pages on your site. Additionally, it allows you to edit the website's posts, pages, design, title, and other settings from web-based pages accessible to logged-in administrators. WordPress is open source software that is available from www.wordpress.org for free.

To have a WordPress website:

- WordPress needs to be installed/set up on your website before it can be used.
- The design of a WordPress website is changed by changing or altering the theme used on the website. You can:
  - Create a custom WordPress theme.
  - Modify an existing WordPress theme.
  - Hire someone to modify an existing WordPress theme.
  - Hire someone to develop a custom WordPress theme.
- More features can be added to WordPress through the use of Plugins. These plugins can be used to add features like the ability to embed YouTube videos into your website or the ability to display products on the website. You can:
  - Search for various plugins that you need in the Plugin

Directory. http://wordpress.org/extend/plugins/

- Modify existing plugins if necessary.

- Hire someone to modify an existing plugin.

- Hire someone to write a plugin from scratch.

- Write a plugin from scratch.

A Blog

If you want to provide advice, reviews, and other relevant information, adding a blog may help bring visitors to your website. If you update the blog fairly frequently (daily or at least once every couple days), a blog may provide reasons for visitors to come to your website and keep visiting your website.

To have a blog:

- You need to find a blogging web application. WordPress can be used as a blogging web application.
- The blogging web application needs to be installed/set up on your website before it can be used.
- The blog's design needs to be customized.
- There is a possibility that you could add additional features to your blog if your blogging software supports plugins.

These aforementioned items can be done by you or you can pay someone else to do them for you.

A Forum/Discussion Board

A forum/discussion board allows users to communicate with one another. It can be used to attract visitors and keep them coming back to post and read other people's responses to their posts.

To have a Forum/Discussion Board:

- You need to find a forum/discussion board web application.
- The forum web application needs to be installed/set up on your website before it can be used.
- The Forum's design needs to be customized. Usually forum designs are called skins, and the skin's files can be modified, for example, to change a logo.
- There is a possibility that you could add additional features to your forum if your forum software supports plugins.

These aforementioned items can be done by you or you can pay someone else to do them for you.

Hosted Shopping Applications

There are services that make it easier for you to sell products online. These services are mostly focused around selling physical products online, and enable you to log in, modify settings, add product information, and sell products.

To get started with a hosted shopping application:

- Register a domain name.
- Sign up for the hosted shopping application service.
- Modify the logo and maybe other elements of the design of your shop.
- Modify your shop's settings like payment settings, tax settings, and other similar settings.
- Add your product information.

Social Networking Applications

Social Networking applications such as FaceBook applications help users connect with their friends on FaceBook. By developing FaceBook applications, you can possibly get in front of an audience and get FaceBook users to virally promote your message to their friends.

For more information about writing a FaceBook application, you can visit http://developers.facebook.com/docs/guides/canvas

To write your own social networking application you need to:
- Start with your documentation plan and start coding. You can:
  - Program your web application yourself if you are familiar with the programming language you want to code it in
  - Outsource the programming of the web application

Whether you modify an existing web application or develop your own, you also need to know how to:
- Upload your web application's files
- Install/Setup your web application

Phone Applications

Phone applications such as iPhone applications are installed to users' iPhones and they enable users to do more with their iPhones. iPhone applications can be sold through the App store, or they can be available for free. You can also embed ads into your apps.

To get started developing iPhone applications visit http://developer.apple.com/programs/ios/

To develop iPhone applications, you need to start with your documentation plan and start coding. You can:

- Program your iPhone application yourself if you are familiar with the programming languages you want to use.
- Outsource the programming of your iPhone application.

If you are still having a hard time estimating the required time and money for your projects, you can write down what you have thought of so far and, if you think the idea might be feasible, you can go on to documenting the idea for development, and use the specifics from documenting it to get more specific about the required tasks, and the required time and money for your projects.

When looking back at the various tasks you have to complete, the website to develop and what not, can you do it?

If there are parts of the development that you do not know how to do or you do not think you can do, you could consider outsourcing those parts. Get quotes from providers for this work and decide if you have the money to get the work done.

Also, for the parts you are developing yourself, do you have the time to complete them?

Determine whether they are worth your time

After estimating the time and money it costs to develop each project in each niche, look at each one and determine which ones are worth it and which ones are not. Try to estimate possible revenue from the projects within each niche, based on an estimate of the price of the products, services, and/or subscriptions you would be selling, the affiliate commissions, the ad revenue, and/or revenue from donations, considering the size of the niche.

Eliminate projects that at first glance do not look feasible.

Choose One

After eliminating projects that do not appear feasible, choose your first project. You can choose your favorite project that you think is feasible, or you could roll a dice or flip a coin to try to randomly choose a project.

Determine Feasibility Example – Project

Tennis

Niche Name

_____

Cost Estimate Total

To Do:

Task Description

Tasked To   Internal or Outsourced

Static Website

Channel Name

_____

Duration Estimate Total

Duration   Cost

List your tasks using the format under To Do. Do this once for the one-time tasks that you have to do to develop your projects and once for the monthly time and costs associated with maintaining that project.

Here is a list of possible tasks and expenses to help you fill out the worksheets. You should be more specific and list the sub-tasks for each of these tasks. Some of these might apply to your projects.

For the Project:

- Developing the website, iPhone applications, social networking applications
- Licensing legal forms (http://www.divstart.com/resources/legalforms)
- Developing products

Ongoing Monthly:

- Domain name (yearly price divided by 12)
- Website hosting
- Email auto-responder service
- Writing the content for an email newsletter
- Responding to email
- Checking for spam/irrelevant posts on discussion sections of the website
- Updating the product of the day
- Promoting the website
- Website maintenance

Determine Feasibility Worksheet - Project

Niche Name _____   **Channel Name** _____

Cost Estimate Total   **Duration Estimate Total**

To Do:

Task Description

Tasked To	Internal or Outsourced	Duration	Cost

Determine Feasibility Worksheet - Monthly

_____   _____

Niche Name   **Channel Name**

_____   _____

Cost Estimate Total   **Duration Estimate Total**

To Do:

Task Description

Tasked To   Internal or Outsourced   Duration   Cost

_____

_____

_____

_____

_____

_____

Task Description

Tasked To   Internal or Outsourced   Duration   Cost

_____

_____

_____

_____

_____

_____

6. Document for Development

In this step you should get more specific about your projects and eventually sketch out your project on paper. If you are developing a web application, you should follow up by describing how the pages interact in a text document in as much detail as possible.

You may want to skip this step, and you might be able to. However, I think this step is important because it lets you get your plans for your project finalized. This helps when it comes to the parts of your project that are outsourced, because if you have detailed plans and descriptions to give to the people you outsource to, it will save them time and thus in turn you should save money.

Now that you have a general idea as to what distribution channels and what niche you want to go into, you can get more specific. First, think of all of the channels you are going to use. Try to think of ways to relate these together. Can users share one user account across these different channels? For each channel, think of what a user would want to see, do, or interact with. Think about it from both an end user viewpoint and your viewpoint. Also, think of ways to integrate that channel into the user's life.

Here are some things you might want to consider before you start.

Simple Design

While you are free to design your distribution channels the way you see fit, I like to keep the designs as simple as possible. Think about it from the standpoint of a theoretical website visitor. If that visitor comes to a website that is cluttered, that visitor may become confused and leave. However, if that visitor is presented with a website that has a clean, uncluttered design that presents the essentials, then that visitor is more likely to understand what the website is about.

Limiting Risk

When you get more specific and document your projects, try to design your projects to limit your risk. Generally speaking, this means thinking about all of the data your projects are collecting and interacting with. Also realize that the data that you do not collect can not be stolen from you because you never collected it in the first place. For example, I do not recommend collecting credit card numbers and storing them on your website. I instead suggest that you send website visitors to another trusted credit card processor's website to collect the credit card numbers, process the transactions and pay you. This way, at least at first, you do not have to be concerned with things like PCI DSS compliance.

Drawing Tips

While you are documenting projects for development, you will be drawing designs for your projects with pencil and paper. Here are some tips:

- Use blank, white, typing paper.

- Draw a box on the paper to represent the bounds of the screen available for that particular distribution channel. Draw your design for that distribution channel inside this box.

- When drawing lines, draw them lightly first because you may want to erase and re-draw them. To draw lines, keep making short movements with your pencil and move the starting position of your pencil along in a row (end of one short line is the start of the second short line) until the line is drawn.

- Draw boxes first to mark the different sections of the page, then describe the sections.

Before documenting projects, it is important to think about your target market. You can refer back to your niche spreadsheets to try to figure out more about your niche demographics. Keep this in mind while you are documenting projects. For example, if you are designing a website for an niche with mostly elderly people, you might want to make the size of the text on the website larger.

An example of documenting projects for development for each distribution channel follows. If you are interested in documenting a static website squeeze page, use the worksheet in that section. Otherwise, use the worksheet at the end of this step for each distribution channel for each niche. Answer the questions on the worksheet first, then start drawing and describing your drawings. Just remember that you can keep re-drawing something until you think it looks good, so don't be afraid to try drawing a unique design for a distribution channel. It might work.

A Static Website

When documenting a static website, the main focus is the design.

You should decide whether this static website is going to be a squeeze page or a regular static website.

Squeeze Page

If you want to make this static website a squeeze page, fill out the worksheets provided below and then draw the website's pages with pencil and paper. The following page is an example squeeze page design.

Squeeze Page

Website Name
OR
Website Logo

Video, Audio, Text information...

Subscribe and
Receive a
Free Downloadable
Report

PDF

Name

Email

Subscribe

Read our Privacy Policy

Links to Legal Documents

Document for Development Example

Tennis

<u>Niche Name</u>

Static Squeeze Page

Channel Name

Documenting Your Ideas:

What are you going to display on the squeeze page to get website visitors to opt-in to your newsletter?

This could possibly be video, audio, or text information.

What are you going to give away for free as an incentive to opt-in to your newsletter?

Possibly a short PDF document providing tips, or possibly a 5 step email course.

What information do you need to collect with the subscribe box?

Name and email address, and possibly other information such as interests.

Basic Site Map:

Fill in the blanks below with the names of the website's pages.

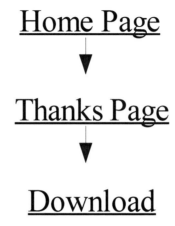

Home Page

Thanks Page

Download

What links are you going to display at the top of your website (linked to from every page)?

Home Page

What links are you going to display at the bottom of your website (linked to from every page)?

Legal Documents, Contact Us

Document for Development Worksheet

Static Squeeze Page

_____

Niche Name   **Channel Name**

Documenting Your Ideas:

What are you going to display on the squeeze page to get website visitors to opt-in to your newsletter?

_____

_____

What are you going to give away for free as an incentive to opt-in to your newsletter?

_____

_____

What information do you need to collect with the subscribe box?

_____

_____

Basic Site Map:

Fill in the blanks below with the names of the website's pages.

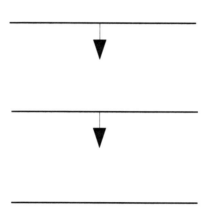

What links are you going to display at the top of your website (linked to from every page)?

_____

_____

What links are you going to display at the bottom of your website (linked to from every page)?

_____

_____

Regular Static Website

I like to start by thinking of the content that needs to be displayed on the website. Then try to think of a simple way of breaking this down into web pages. What content needs to be displayed on what page?

I like to then think of the sections that I want on the website. These sections could include:

- Navigation – a listing of links to other main pages on the website
- Content – the main information on that page of the website
- Logo – text or an image representing the name of the website or the company name
- Legal Navigation – links to legal documents such as terms of service or privacy policy

You can then either find a website template and write about and draw how you want to modify it or you can design the website yourself. To do this, I try to think of how I want to arrange the website's sections on a page. There are many different possibilities. Also, to have consistency in your website design across the pages on your website, many pages on your website can have similar sections with different information.

Static Website Site Map

Home Page

Products

Services
- Service 1
- Service 2

About Us

Contact Us

Legal Documents
- Disclaimer
- Terms of Use
- Privacy Policy
- Anti-Spam Policy
- Compensation Disclosure
- others

Static Website

Website Name or Website Logo

Home | Products | Services | About Us | Contact Us

Website Content

Links to legal Documents

Web Applications

I like to start with the big picture. Think of the end user. Think of the niche. Think of the monetization strategies you plan on integrating into this web application.

Web applications can have many features such as:
- Standard features
- Information or training delivery features
- Social features
- Administrative features

Standard features

Standard features include things like:
- Forms where information is inputted
- Displaying information from a database

Information or training delivery features

Information or training delivery features include things like:
- FAQ pages

- Product description pages

- Video tutorial pages

- Tutorials

Social features

Social features include things like:

- Instant messaging features where website members can chat with each other

- Messaging capabilities where messages can be sent between website users

- Forums where users can post messages and reply to other user's messages.

Administrative features

Administrative features include things like:

- Editing website settings online

- Editing website content online

- Managing users

- Other features commonly found within areas of web applications only accessible to web application administrators.

These administrative features are commonly put into areas of the website called admin panels. To show an example of an admin panel, here is what the WordPress version 3 admin panel looks like.

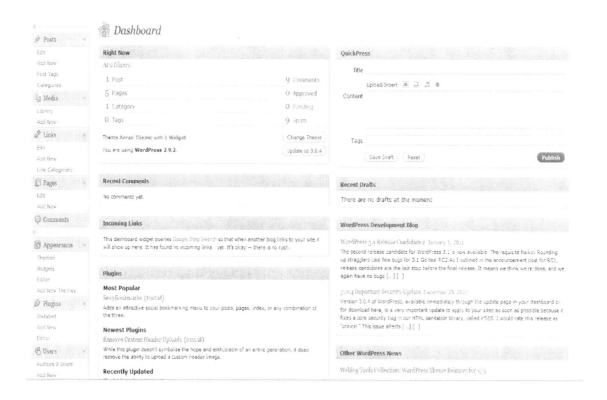

Also realize that these admin panels should be separate from the other pages on the site map. I suggest you create a separate site map for the admin panel.

First decide on the feature that is the core of your web application and keep adding features to it.

- Does your web application list products that your company has for sale and provide descriptions of these products?
- Does your web application allow people to interact with each other?
- Does your web application help people learn something
- Does your web application provide a service to people like converting videos from one format to another?
- Is your web application a blog?
- Is your web application a forum?
- Is your web application mostly for displaying content online

Then determine what features are necessary to make these main features possible.

For starters, most of these features require:

- User accounts
- Displaying information from some type from a database
- Search capabilities (searching for products, blog posts, etc...)
- Users sending information to the website, which is then stored in the database

- Admin pages to manage the user accounts and the information in the database

You can then think of other features that you might want to add:
- Adding product reviews to a shopping website
- Adding instant messaging capabilities to a forum

Also consider that many larger websites offer services called APIs (Application Programming Interfaces) that let you use their data in your web applications. Websites like these have API's:
- Google (http://code.google.com/more/)
- Amazon (http://aws.amazon.com/ - products tab)
- eBay (http://developer.ebay.com/)
- Facebook (http://developers.facebook.com/docs/guides/web)

Try to think of what pages are necessary. The following pages are necessary for most of these features:
- Home page
- Log-in page
- Log-out page
- Page to display information from the database
- Search results page

- Admin panel pages:
  - User management pages
  - Information management pages

There might be other pages that are necessary to specific web applications such as:

- Shopping cart page
- Checkout page
- Order successful page
- Page for users to input information
- Page to display settings that users can change

You might not think of every single feature or page before you start documenting your web application, however by documenting the web application, you will probably find gaps in your ideas that you can then fill. You could also create a mind map to show the visual connections within an application.

Start with the home page. Decide what information a visitor to your website wants to see before using your web application. Also realize that web applications can use squeeze pages. Thus you could have a form of a squeeze page as your home page. Probably the best example of a squeeze page as a home page for a web application is Facebook's website at http://www.facebook.com Also, squeeze pages are sometimes used while a web application is being developed or during the launch of a web application. An example of this is when you sign up for an invite to use a web application.

Start by drawing the home page with pencil and paper. Then draw the pages that the home page links to and the pages that those pages link to and so on until the pages of the website are drawn.

Then think about the admin panel. What information needs to be managed? Draw the pages that make up the admin panel.

If necessary, write about how the pages interact with each other or how a feature of the web application works.

The following is an example of the documentation for a few pages of a web application.

Web Application Site Map

Home Page

The Tabs to
- Videos
- Articles
- News
- Products

update the content
on the home page
to display only
that type of content.

Legal Documents
- Disclaimer
- Terms of Use
- Privacy Policy
- Anti-Spam Policy
- Compensation Disclosure
- Others

119

Web Application Example

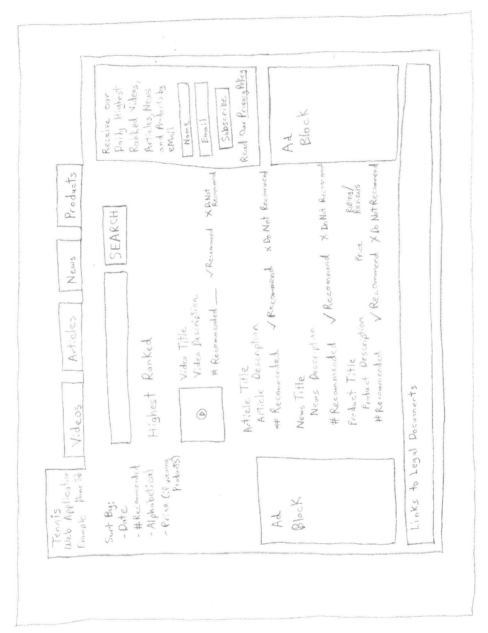

Tenn's
Web Application
Example Home Page

Videos | Articles | News | Products

Sort By:
- Date
- #Recommended
- Alphabetical
- Price (if we one Products)

SEARCH

Highest Ranked

Video Title
Video Description
Recommended ___ √ Recommend X Not Recommend

Article Title
Article Description
#Recommended √ Recommend x Do Not Recommend

News Title
News Description
#Recommended √ Recommend X Do Not Recommend

Product Title
Product Description   Price   Rating/Reviews
#Recommend √ Recommend X Do Not Recommend

Receive Our
Daily Highest
Ranked Videos,
Articles, News
and Products by
eMail

Name
Email
Subscribe

Read Our Privacy Policy

Ad
Block

Ad
Block

Links to Legal Documents

If you want to get more detailed in your planning, you can plan the database for the web application.

To plan the database for the web application, think about the information and how the information is pulled from a database and used on the website. Identify similar information and group it together. For example, you can group together product information. You can also group together forum posts and/or blog posts. You can also group together user information.

Think about how you would display this information in a spreadsheet with the columns being the type of information and the information being displayed one item to a row.

You can also split up spreadsheets to make multiple spreadsheets out of one spreadsheet if necessary. This is necessary when the same information is duplicated in multiple rows in the spreadsheet. For example, the name of a product category should be separate from the spreadsheet listing the products themselves because more than one product can be in a category. The same thing is true for orders, since more than one user can order more than one item. In these cases, multiple spreadsheets need to be created. A spreadsheet needs to be created to store the user and the order number and possibly the date of the order and the total price at checkout. A spreadsheet needs to be created to store the order number and each product in the order.

Add a column at the beginning of each table for a unique number to uniquely identify each row in the table. This unique identifier can be used in other spreadsheets to uniquely identify a specific row in that spreadsheet to link the spreadsheets together.

A WordPress Website

When documenting a WordPress website, the main focus is the theme.

You can visit http://www.wordpress.org/extend/themes to see existing WordPress themes that could be modified or a WordPress theme could be developed from scratch.

WordPress Website Site Map

Home Page

Products

Blog

About Us

Contact Us

Legal Documents
- Disclaimer
- Terms of Use
- Privacy Policy
- Anti-Spam Policy
- Compensation Disclosure
- Others

A WordPress Website

Title / Logo

Home
Products
Blog
About Us
Contact Us

Recent Comments

Links to legal documents

Welcome Page

Subscribe to our Newsletter

Name

Email

Subscribe

Read Our Privacy Policy

Ads

A Blog

When documenting a Blog, the main focus is the theme.

Depending on the blogging software you plan on using, you may be able to find existing themes, or you could develop your own.

Blog Site Map

Home Page

Search

Older Posts

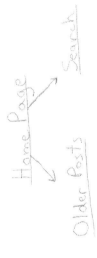

Legal Documents
- Disclaimer
- Terms of Use
- Privacy Policy
- Anti Spam Policy
- Compensation Disclosure
- Others

Blog

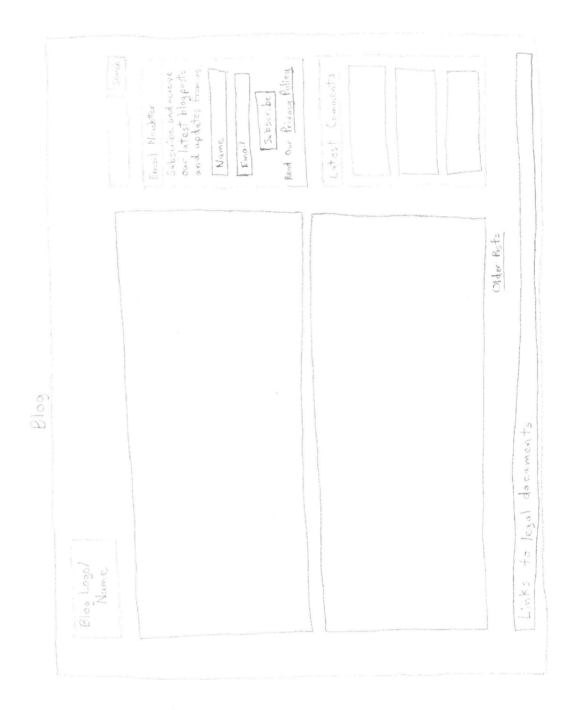

Blog Logo/
Name

Email Newsletter

Subscribe and receive
our latest blogposts
and updates from us

Name

Email

Subscribe

Read Our Privacy Policy

Latest Comments

Older Posts

Links to legal documents

A Forum/Discussion Board

When documenting a Forum/Discussion Board, the main focus is the skin. A skin usually consists of a logo, images to be used instead of the existing forum icons, a color scheme, and other design elements of the forum.

Depending on what Forum/Discussion Board software you plan on using, you may be able to modify an existing skin, or develop your own.

Forum / Discussion Board Site Map

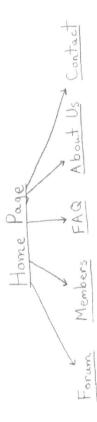

Home Page

Forum

Members

FAQ

About Us

Contact

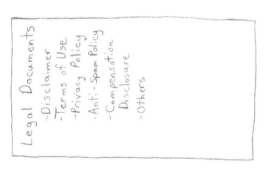

Legal Documents
- Disclaimer
- Terms of Use
- Privacy Policy
- Anti-Spam Policy
- Compensation Disclosure
- Others

Forum | Discussion Board

Forum Name

Home   Forum   Members   FAQ   About Us   Contact

User Name   Password   Login   Register
☐ Remember Me?

Search
Advanced Search

Forum Name

Section Title

Forum Image   Forum Name
Forum Description
Forums Within Forum:

LastPost
Title and Link
Date

Threads:
Posts:

Recent Posts
Post Name
Post Description
Read More

Sponsors

Links to legal documents

Hosted Shopping Applications

Hosted shopping applications usually come with themes that you can select. You might be able to modify these themes, create one from scratch or get someone else to create a theme for you.

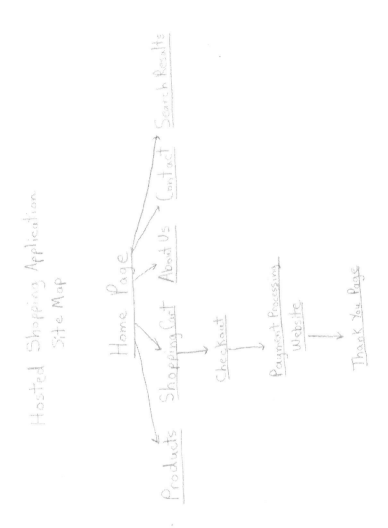

133

Hosted Shopping Application

Site Name

Products | About Us | Contact

Search

Welcome Message

Receive our Deal of the Day by email
Name
Email
Subscribe
Read Our Privacy Policy

Cart
Total
Checkout

Categories

Featured Products

Links to legal documents

Social Networking Applications

Developing a Social Networking Application is going to be similar to developing a web application. However, because you are building on top of a social platform, you have extra features that your app can use. To see some of these extra features, look at Facebook's documentation for Facebook Query Language at http://developers.facebook.com/docs/reference/fql/ Facebook Markup language at http://developers.facebook.com/docs/reference/fbml/ Dialog Overview at http://developers.facebook.com/docs/reference/dialogs/ and the JavaScript SDK at http://developers.facebook.com/docs/reference/javascript/

Social Networking Application Site Map

Main Page

The user can input who won against a particular friend.

Before this can affect the rankings, the other friend has to confirm that result.

The rankings for all of that user's friends who use the application are displayed below the confirm results section

Legal Documents
- Disclaimer
- Terms of Use
- Privacy Policy
- Anti-Spam Policy
- Compensation Disclosure
- Others

Social Networking Application

Tennis App

Input Results

You   vs   Friend in first LH ▼

[Winner]   [Winner]

Confirm Results

You won against Friend A   [Yes] [No]
You lost against Friend B   [Yes] [No]

Rankings
1 Friend B
2 Friend C
3 You
4 Friend A
5 Friend D
6 Friend E
7 Friend F
8 Friend G
9 Friend H
10 Friend I
   →

Phone Applications

Documenting a Phone Application is going to be similar to documenting a web application. You will need to draw out the design for your phone application on paper. I suggest you start with the main screen of the application you want to create, and then draw the screens that the main screen links to.

Phone Application Map

Main Screen

Add Place   Help   Place Listing

Phone Application

Main Screen

[_____] [Search]

Display Only: Higher Than [★★★★★]
□ Lit □ Not Lit

Map

[+ Add Place]   [Help]

Add Place

Near
[Address_____]
City: [_____]
State: [_____▼]
Zip: [_____]

□ Lit   □ Not Lit

[Add Place]

[Back]

Help

Help

How to use the app...

[Back]

Place Near
Address
City, State Zip

Lit

Avg Rating: ★★★
Add Rating [★★★★★▼]
Comments: [ADD]
[_____]

Other Ratings
★★★★
- - - - - - - - - - - - -
Comments

★★★
Comments

★★★★★
Comments

[Back]

Document for Development Example

Tennis

Niche Name

Static Website

Channel Name

Documenting Your Ideas:

What products, services, subscriptions, advertisements, affiliate products, or donate buttons need to be listed on the website?

List them here.

What general information needs to be listed on the website? Contact information? About us information?

List it here.

What else needs to be listed on the website? Specials? Certifications? Credentials?

List it here.

What links are you going to display at the top of your website (linked to from every page)?

List links here.

What links are you going to display at the bottom of your website (linked to from every page)?

List links here.

Site Map:

Draw a site map of the website on a blank sheet of paper.

Site Design:

Get a pencil and a sheet of paper for each page on your website, take your ideas for sections, and start drawing how you want these sections to look.

Document for Development Worksheet

_____   _____

Niche Name   **Channel Name**

Documenting Your Ideas:

What products, services, subscriptions, advertisements, affiliate products, or donate buttons need to be listed on the website?

_____

_____

What general information needs to be listed on the website? Contact information? About us information?

_____

_____

What else needs to be listed on the website? Specials? Certifications? Credentials?

_____

_____

What links are you going to display at the top of your website (linked to from every page)?

_____

_____

_____

What links are you going to display at the bottom of your website (linked to from every page)?

_____

_____

_____

Site Map:

Draw a site map of the website on a blank sheet of paper.

Site Design:

Get a pencil and a sheet of paper for each page on your website, take your ideas for sections, and start drawing how you want these sections to look.

7. Obtain Domain Name and Website Hosting

You now need to obtain a domain name and website hosting.

To find domain names:

1. I usually start with the main concepts behind the website such as:

   - Your Niche

   - Your Industry

   - The Category of Products You Sell

   - Your Business Location (If you are also an offline business)

   - Positive Adjectives You Want Associated with Your Site
     Ex: Quality
     You can get ideas for these concepts from your niche
     spreadsheets.
     If you are having a hard time thinking of a word, you can try
     the Tip of My Tongue app at
     http://chir.ag/projects/tip-of-my-tongue/

2. I take these words and find synonyms. To find synonyms, you could
   use a website like http://www.thesaurus.com or
   http://www.visuwords.com/

3. I try to mix these words together in ways that make sense.

4. I check the availability of these combinations of words. For more information visit http://www.divstart.com/resources/domains

5. I keep a list of the available words.

6. I choose the combination that I think best fits the project.

Suggestions:

- Make sure the .com extension is available in whatever combination of words you try to register. Register at least the .com

- Try to keep your combination of words as short as possible, while still fitting the project. Try not to choose three words when two will do.

- Try to keep the combination of words to two to three words.

- Think about the general thoughts and feelings associated with the words in your combination of words. Are these aligned with your business? For example, cheap might not be appropriate because people might think that cheap things are very low quality and fall apart. Words such as inexpensive, bargain, deal, discount, and low price might be more appropriate.

- See if you can find other words in your combination of words. For example, you probably want to avoid combinations of words that have cuss words in between two or more words, when the words are strung together as they are in domain names.

- Make sure the domain name is pronounceable.

- Make sure that most people can correctly spell the domain name.

- Make sure you are correctly spelling the words in the domain name. For example, you do not want to register your main domain name with misspelled words, when your business name includes the words spelled correctly. However, you can also register misspelled combinations of your words so that no one else can register them and possibly detract from or compete with your business.

- Check to see if both the singular and plural versions of all of the words in the combinations of words are available.

- Check to see if the combination of words with – dashes between every word is available. You can register your combination of words with dashes between every word so that no one else can register it and possibly detract from or compete with your business.

- Check to see how many extensions are available in your combination of words and, if they are not available, who has the other extensions. You can register different extensions of your combination of words so that no one else can register them and possibly detract from or compete with your business.

- Check if the words in your combination of words are available in a different order. For example check if websiteyour.com is available if your combination of words is yourwebsite.com You can register different combinations of your words so that no one else can register them and possibly detract from or compete with your business.

- Check to see if the combination of words you want to resister are trademarked. Visit http://www.uspto.gov/ and click on Search Marks under the Trademarks section and see if your combination of words with and/or without spaces have any live trademarks. If your combination of words are trademarked in a category similar to what you want to do, I would suggest finding a different combination of words, because it may cause problems in the future.

- Search the exact combination of words using the External Keyword Tool at https://adwords.google.com/select/KeywordToolExternal to see if it is a popular combination of words. Having the exact combination of words of a search query in a domain name will probably help you rank higher in the search engines for that exact combination of words. If this combination of words is searched often, this could result in more website visitors. Additionally, if the words you use are the title of a page on http://www.wikipedia.org you could check to see how many visitors that wikipedia page is getting by visiting http://stats.grok.se/

- If you want to make sure you can get your domain name as a username on major social networking websites, you could visit http://www.usernamecheck.com/

Website hosting:

Website hosting is used to host your website's files. There are different types of website hosting depending on what type of website you want to host, the type of content on your website (text, audio, video, etc...) and how many people visit your website every month. To determine what type of website hosting you need for your projects visit http://www.divstart.com/resources/hosting

Obtain Domain Name and Website Hosting Example

Niche Name: <u>Tennis</u>   **Channel Name:** <u>Static Website</u>

Words:

Positive Adjectives: fast, quick, pro

Location Words: List location words separated by commas.

Types of Products: List product type words separated by commas.

Niche Words: List niche words separated by commas.

Domains:

Domain Name	Extensions Available	Number of Characters
Tennis	.com .org	19

Obtain Domain Name and Website Hosting Worksheet

_____   _____

Niche Name   **Channel Name**

Words:

Positive Adjectives: _____

_____

Location Words: _____

_____

Type of Products: _____

_____

Niche Words: _____

_____

Other Words: _____

_____

Domains:

Domain Name	Extensions Available	Number of Characters

Index

CPSIA information can be obtained at www.ICGtesting.com
Printed in the USA
LVOW07s0030121213

364961LV00001B/14/P